CW01468515

CHAOS

CHAOS

POETRY ANTHOLOGY

SELECTED POEMS

PATRICIAN PRESS
MANNINGTREE

First published as a paperback edition by Patrician Press 2020

E-book edition published by Patrician Press 2020

Copyright for Chaos Poetry Anthology © Patrician Press 2020

Copyright for each text contributed remains with the author.

All rights reserved. No part of this document may be reproduced or transmitted in any form or by any means, electronic, mechanical, photocopying, recording, or otherwise, without prior written permission of Patrician Press.

British Library Cataloguing in Publication Data. A catalogue record for this book is available from the British Library.

ISBN paperback edition 978-1-9997030-3-5

CHAOS POETRY ANTHOLOGY

EDITED BY ANNA JOHNSON

Published by Patrician Press Collective 2020

Refuge Is a Taxi; Something Human; Evensong; The Photo; The Decision; Crossing Borders, The Border; first published by Patrician Press in the Refugees and Peacekeepers Anthology (2017). Take Back Control; The Conjuring; DNA; Je Suis Européen; first published by Patrician Press in the My Europe Anthology (2018). Some Start Fires; The Cowboy with the Calcium Spur; first published by Patrician Press in the Tempest Anthology (2019).

"The futility of action does not absolve one from the failure to act."

The Last Magician **Janette Turner Hospital**

Contents

Introduction

Patrician Press has published three anthologies since 2017: *Refugees and Peacekeepers*, *My Europe* and *Tempest*. All three collections are, as their titles suggest, attempts to understand events which have gripped our attention and divided public opinion: the refugee crisis, our membership of the EU, Brexit, and the juggernaut of climate change in an era of global political turmoil.

Chaos is the latest anthology in this series, a prescient title given the pandemic now engulfing us.

It is a collection of poems, some taken from earlier anthologies, some newly minted; it records and reacts to the crises we have lived through over the past five years, a period of polarisation when light and darkness have seemed in constant contention.

In the introduction to *Refugees and Peacekeepers* I talked about the boundaries that divide us and the narratives of intolerance that reinforce them. *My Europe* reflected on how we are manipulated by unreliable narratives and fake news, and *Tempest* mooted that our inability to acknowledge others' ideas has caused paralysis in our democracy and a rupture in society.

Chaos sees us struggling to find a path back to normality. World leaders' metaphors are martial, as if they might beat back coronavirus by the act of declaring war on it: doctors and nurses are on the 'frontline'. This kind of language is rousing, but dangerous; there should be no need for heroism in properly resourced hospitals, no need for sacrifice if staff are properly protected.

In some ways history is repeating itself; Daniel Defoe's A *Journal of a Plague Year* (1722) describes the wealthy thundering down the road to Oxford and safety, whilst the poor take on the riskiest essential jobs – searching, guarding, nursing, burying. Then, as now, plague was not an equal opportunities killer but made hay in the economic margins of society.

As I write, the Home Secretary's bill to end 'low skilled' immigration has cleared its first hurdle in the Commons. Anyone earning less than £20,000 will not get a visa to work in the U.K. All those who have cared for our elderly, delivered our food and goods, cleaned our hospitals, all those for whom we were encouraged to cheer on our door steps, have had their contribution valued at nought. We are told that they are not 'the people we need to drive our economy forward'. Many of these workers are immigrants. Many people used their Brexit vote to keep them out; many of us – including our prime minister – now owe them our lives. We are assured that the new points system is 'firmer, fairer, simpler', but it does not recognise selflessness or compassion, or any quality that is not now a quantifiable 'skill'.

There has been an outpouring of creativity in response to this pandemic; front windows have become exhibition spaces. The artist Jeremy Deller was inspired to issue a poster reading, 'Thank God for Immigrants' in the hope that this, too, would be hung in front windows. The money raised went to Refugee Action and the Trussell food banks. Clearly, Deller expressed what a lot of people were thinking, but not saying.

In difficult times, then, we turn to Art; poetry, in particular, is one of the pithiest ways to process events that seem extreme. When life and politicians' verbs are conditional, and we don't know how the future will look, poetry gives voice to our feelings. When words are deployed to whip up fear, to accuse, to isolate, it can be a refuge. As M W Bewick puts it, 'writing quivers in the small spaces' but it is disproportionately powerful.

I hope that *Chaos* provides a mirror for strange times; it was certainly produced in extremis and runs the gamut from rage to love, grief to hope. There is poetry here that restores humanity to the refugees who would otherwise be effaced. There is nostalgic verse about the 'magic' of travelling freely across Europe. There is poetry that reminds us that we are all alike under the skin. There is an elegy for the toddler whose body was washed up on a Turkish beach in 2016. There is George Szirtes' powerful reminder of what being European means.

The following poems are new and deserve special mention.

Toll Out, Sad Bells, the second of two poems by Attila the Stockbroker, is a lament for the 'faithless coldness of the times'; every line rings out the pain, the anger and the grief of leaving Europe. The final line, 'Toll in the heist that is to be,' alludes to the theft of our future by the same pack of unscrupulous chancers now running the country.

As our climate reaches a tipping point, many of us are

enjoying the clear skies and cleaner air that are two positive aspects of lockdown. M W Bewick's *Talkin Ramblin' Anthropocene Poetry Blues* opines, bluntly, 'We are not clever, /Tear things apart. Wear things out.'

Humanity has come to a reckoning; on a domestic scale, the author had to move his crocosmia 'before the heat dug in,' but as a species we must face 'our bloody anthropocene come'.

May You Live... by Mark Brayley focuses on the candour of lockdown communication when our responses are, 'raw, uncut and justified'; we 'spew' our words into the 'void' that lies between us and 'speculate the end/to hate.' It is a function of our apartness, perhaps, that 'we grow unseen /with hope/of unity'.

Hunkered Doon by Christine de Luca celebrates memory as a tool for consolation when our spirits are 'twisted or tangled'; we can find 'summer's sunrise saved/ in the loft of memory' and wrap it around ourselves.

The Truth of Us by Martin Johnson is a delightfully succinct assessment of life, 'Stanzas of happiness/Couplets of gloom.' Dispassionate, witty, upbeat.

In *Wild Isolation*, Martin Reed notices what happens, 'Behind-the-houses Beside-the-road,' when the people are kept in and the roads are empty. In the quiet, 'a bird flies over and the world blinks,' a tremor of awareness felt across continents.

In *Untitled*, Philip Terry muses on how innocuously a tragedy can begin, 'A slight cough at which no one bats an eyelid.' *Message Clear* by contrast is a riff on how easily language and truth shift through use from the edgy to the provocative, from the elusive to – finally – the terrifying; 'Steer Algebraic>>Convey the Voracious>>Sacrifice Life.'

In these uncertain times, when we must all sometimes wonder which new apocalypse will come galloping over the horizon, I hope there is enough in these pages to console, entertain and feed the spirit.

Anna Johnson

TAKE BACK CONTROL

ATTILA THE STOCKBROKER

You tell me how you've suffered since the closure.
I see the pain and sadness in your eyes.
I feel your anger at our country's leaders
Who offer only platitudes and lies.
At gigs I hear so many of these stories.
All different, but the message is the same.
You're sick to death of scheming politicians.
No longer going to play their poxy game.

The referendum was your chance. You took it.
They told you we'd be taking back control.
Control of jobs and factories and borders:
A revolution wrapped up in a poll.
The EU is a ghastly corporate bully.
Cheap labour and big profits at its core.
I understand why you voted for Brexit:
One chance to strike a blow in the class war.

But it wasn't the EU who shut your pit down
And sent Met thugs rampaging through your street.
They didn't close your hospitals and workshops,
Smash down your union to brave defeat.
No EU diktat caused the housing crisis,
The poll tax, bedroom tax or zero hours.
No, all of these were brought in by the Tories –
And soon those bastards will have brand new powers.

So let's take back control with strong trade unions
And let's take back control and organise.
Take back control of pub and school and workplace
And counter all the endless media lies.
Take back control as we all stand together.
No scapegoating and no divide and rule.
The future is unwritten, and it's daunting.
Please don't let UKIP take you for a fool.

TOLL OUT, SAD BELL

ATTILA THE STOCKBROKER

Toll out, sad bell, to the sad sky,
The flying cloud, the frosty light:
The dream is dying in the night:
Toll out, sad bell, and let it die.
Toll out the young, toll in the old:
A red face in a bungalow.
The dream is going, let it go.
Toll out the warm, toll in the cold.

Toll in the grief that saps the mind
For those that here we'll see no more;
Toll in the feud of rich and poor,
Toll in controls for all mankind.
Toll out a slowly dying cause,
That sought to end our nations' strife;
Toll in a different way of life,
With baser manners, pettier laws.

Toll in the want, the care, the sin,
The faithless coldness of the times;
Toll out, toll out my mournful rhymes:
The wandering minstrel won't get in.
Toll in false pride in place and blood,
The civic slander and the spite;
Toll out the love of truth and right,
Toll out the common love of good.

Toll in old shapes of foul disease;
Toll in the narrowing lust of gold;

Toll in the thousand wars of old,
Toll out the thousand years of peace.
Toll out the valiant man and free,
The larger heart, the kindlier hand;
Toll in the darkness of the land,
Toll in the heist that is to be.

REFUGE IS A TAXI

PEN AVEY

A city gent gets into Basim's taxi cab.
Speaks on his mobile—never misses a beat.
A Rolex peeks from beneath
His gold-cufflinked Paul Smith shirt.
The fare comes to ten pounds
And a tenner is tendered.
Still, Basim smiles and wishes
His customer a nice evening.

Later that night two girls
Giggle behind freshly hennaed hands.
They speak of boys they like
Boldly in Urdu; never guessing
That their lowly driver speaks eleven languages—five fluently.
They tip him two pounds.
He could say goodbye in their mother tongue
But he is far too polite.

Between jobs Basim studies.
He wants to learn how to fix cars,
To own his own garage, maybe. One day
He wishes to get married, start a family.
His hopes are simple, yet complex,
But dreaming is enough to spur him on.
He has come this far—there is no edge
To this land of opportunity.

Yet in the dark they come again
To wrap his hands around the
Cold, hard barrel of an assault rifle.
Sweat stings his eyes, and he wipes it away
As he watches out for the enemy.
His friend is shot through the cheek–
Ragged flesh exposing teeth
As a wasted life ebbs away.

Basim runs, his heart thumps,
Rasping breath, blood in his throat.
He hides a while in the bleak mountains.
He weeps, he prays.
He wakes–the holy words still on his lips,
Thanking Allah for answered prayers.
Removing the sweat-soaked pillow slip to air,
Basim hums as he heads outside,
For the freedom of his next fare.

SOMETHING HUMAN

REBECCA BALFOURTH

They say charity starts at home.
They say home's where the heart is
and I find my heart can cross borders
to sprawl on the couch of a person
I've never known.
By virtue of a red passport,
I've grown in places not my own,
had the privilege to call them home
and left my heart lying around
casual, careless.
I can't imagine what it's like to be
placeless, faceless, nameless,
a story in another place's papers.
To be bordered in and boarded up –
I've never pleaded with strangers
to let me in to a cold and foreign nation
where I feel unwelcome,
derided and despised for trying
to save my life.
I've never fled.
I've never seen one person dead
at the hands of another.
Whatsoever you do to the least of my brothers,
that you do unto me
and I can believe that's true.
So if charity starts at home,

and if home's where the heart is,
my heart goes out to strangers
like a note in a bottle, its message
something human
something strong.

SOME START FIRES

M W BEWICK

For the world's hot air is waste, effluent,
and it dries voices to an earnest hush,
a warning that something approaches,
quick as a boomerang, fathomless but clear,
the return of some hard horror of which
we remain only casually aware.

The top man at the office lifts a hand,
fills his glass at the water cooler, casts
away profit warnings, checks his mirror,
mutters something about resilience,
while the heat chokes up his vacant city
until it can hardly breathe.
This, already.

This silence – our silence – is what we hear,
a mouthed howl of loss, already knowing
the shouts in the street are gone, no witnesses
left in the empty parks, for those who can
are jailed indoors playing waiting games
with the nights of fever-pitched sleep to come.
To be cool, to be cooled, is to be rich.
The otherfolk slowly tread the concrete
while a hospital's heat wards fill with the poor,
the aged, the sick, the overweight, the frail,
and the victims of the surge in urban crime

trapped by the toxic city,
city of fire.

Temperatures hit 50 by dead degrees.
In Australia, the bush fires start in winter,
edge towards the cities of New South Wales
where swimming pools offer safety for cash.
Afternoon work becomes an outlawed pursuit
in Kuwait, where they've started harvesting fog.

The burning sky is deserted of birds,
asphalt melts under a Red-Listed lizard,
and your plastic office glass is flimsy
but corporate water is nice and cool.
Compromises will be made, and we must
escape from blaze after
blaze after blaze.

Some people start those fires, is what they say.
And oh, they really do, they really do.

TALKIN' RAMBLIN' ANTHROPOCENE POETRY BLUES

M W BEWICK

The message in a bottle stranded on a beach,
sperm whales and cargoes of timber, shored,
starfish in their thousands,
palm oil and brine, the osmotic potential thereof, in the sea,
ghost ships drifting to land, life rafts unused, crew nowhere
– headlines washing back up at our feet –
a tangle of plastic, nets, commercial catches, but not
the nets' own narratives, spelled out in strings
of hydrocarbons, metaphors in petrochemicals,
the sun, rain, the rest, diminished, adjectival.

We pretend like it's all random.

For today the moon is a broken button
on a blue and freshly ironed shirt.
An aeroplane makes a needle and thread,
everything darned, nothing properly fixed.
We make do.
And the prospect of another day in an office is better,
wanting heating when it's cold,
huddled on trains,
turning up the volume in a cockpit of a car
caught in a bottleneck on the edge of a town.

Fuming. Exhausted.
Trying to get home.
Trying to forget.

And it was last summer, just gone,
and we moved the crocosmia before the heat dug in.
They never stood a chance.
Last winter, drier than the Med.
I should have cut the leaves back to the ground
but instead watched them yellow like I knew they would.
We do this; then nothing.
My mother calls them monbretia.
Prefers the old names.
Reminds her in sound of another country
where the air is cool and clear.
I tell her they come from the grasslands of Sudan.
Silence.

No one can sustain narrative
as long as is wanted. As long as is needed.
We crack. Opt out.
Seek alternatives or light relief.
We agree it's best to agree that the hours have come undone.
Fissures come to ice and rock.
Glaciers come and go.
Time won't tack itself down.
Our own lives are non-linear,
become a thing of chance,
where an asteroid might end debate.
Let's find another star for our lebensraum,
little fascists that we are.

Let's leave it at that.
We are not clever.
Tear things apart. Wear things out.
All that we need is simple.

Our words must all be left-aligned. 12 point
Times New Roman.
As much as an indent gives us shivers.

            How's
                        That

                                    Then?

Writing is the hardest thing.
Not words, words are everywhere.
Writing quivers in the small spaces.
Poets scratch it out but wash their hands straight after.

Like in a polished Oxfordshire town where a pent-up woman
takes my arm and tells me it's good I care about climate
change.
It's not too late, she says,
her husband nods, hen-ish,
then heads towards the pub toilet in early autumn,
grumbles something about
bloody paintings in a cave
bloody coins in a muddy field
bloody roads and tumbled walls
bloody forests all hacked down
bloody iron and bloody steel
bloody ships and aeroplanes
bloody guns and bloody bombs

bloody power for bloody homes
bloody plastic and foil and
bloody chicken bones.

Can our violence be slow?
How slow?
For this is what I am thinking
about what we have done,
our bloody anthropocene come.

RIDE THE WAVES

THERENA BLAIR

It's time to escape to the hills

Run away from:
self-denying pills, exaggerated bills,
tablets, false frills and information towers that
expel human powers.

Having us online for hours,
blocking our natural intelligence.

See –
now we have no defence.

No sense
Can't smell, can't taste
Soon no rights
Turned-off lights
No flights, no race –
To get out of here!

Running away from each other in public
Get back!
We're too close!
6-foot rule, or 6-foot under!

Hardly do we conversate.

Tongue tied behind masks,
a raised brow in acknowledgement,
Humanity – absent

How long will the silence last?

No evidence we've been out as our prints hibernate in gloves.

Please sanitise
Oh yes – and sanitise again!

That's the new expression of love.

Now go home,
Stay in and saves lives!

No commute!

Just unlimited data from your broadband provider
Added in gest' of good will.
Assisting to expand your library on Netflix during your time
incarcerated

(Quarantine and chill)

While they sign on dotted lines the demise of your freedom
Your voice
Your life
Your will.

Your days are numbered
No longer the place you once knew,
Uncertain to what we're permitted to do

So we stand...

Only at 8pm to applaud NHS soldiers.
Every Thursday night as another street light
is swiftly replaced by a giant wand of distraction.

Missing in action are the minds of many.
So much white noise
We won't hear the penny... drop
To your knees
You submissive being!

They won't stop, as you never stop:

Roaming, cyber-liking, cell phoning, mind droning over the
catalogue of box sets you've watched, over the insta fix you
get from sexy pics, nude hips, diamanté speckled homes, lust
and temptations an inbox of lies, a ring pushed aside as you
make new cyber "friends" with
hey, hello, hi... is anyone in?

Screenshots, religious quotes and quarantined memes, copy
and pasting that pseudo life –
Your dream.

It's time to wake up to the tricks before it's too late to fix...

Hello... anybody there?
Does anybody care?

Isolation has you alone waving down the phone to loved ones,
with tears rolling, knowing *they're* controlling your every
move.

Alexa,

please tell me when we'll wake up and stop laying down to save them while they continue to kill us and fuel us with sanitised lies.

Social distancing us from *love* and any *real* feelings as we channel into how **great** technology is and if it wasn't for Wi-Fi We'd never be able to attend the streamed funeral of **Our** beloved old **rights**.

No ties to the truth
Smoked glass, can't see through it
Just Bluetooth hi-fives
Saying *goodbye*
to life as we once knew it.

THE COWBOY WITH THE CALCIUM SPUR

MARK BRAYLEY

The mother, proud but post-natal, tired and torn,
sat at the side of the white jailhouse cowboy cot
and sighed a stifled smile for her infant newborn.
The father was out, celebrating his white hot

virility with good scotch and better wishes.
Alone, at home, the new mother was not to know
that simple fear for the future diminishes
us all. How, in time, will her newborn baby grow?

Will he be a cowboy with a calcium spur,
brittle, SANE, fit for office, and medically
exempt from the poor's selective service,
yes sir, but, no, not exempt from golf? Momentarily,

the mother looks at the book, Baby and Child Care.
Despite her well-stuck fears, she knows that she knows best
and the justification will be found right there
on page sixty-eight. Spock spoke for the dispossessed

one hundred, two hundred or five hundred thousand.
With no force, and no violence but otherwise
the permissive men and women across the land
proved just too pampered to permit their own demise.

MAY YOU LIVE...

MARK BRAYLEY

Let your response be raw,
uncut and justified.

In lieu of things to do,
we talk
and words flow
and come
and go
and so our remembered soul
holds this moment.
We speak
to tell the future
of how we held
this moment;
this tome of time
between us
when we were all apart.

Everything before is null
and void.
The void that we cannot touch
between us
comes to rush to hope
and, believe us,
we speculate the end
to hate.

If we leave
the house, we queue
and, on our return,
we cue our words;
spew them through
the void.

While unknown numbers grow,
we know that we will
be free. Unknown
in time and history
we grow unseen
with hope
of unity.

THE CONJURING

CATHERINE COLDSTREAM

The bus we took was
Magic. Wrapped in
Donkey jackets we
Sat out the froth and foam
Of nights on the close edge of
Someone else's world,
In transit.

Coins in our pockets
were cold as pebbles
to our fingertips,
and rattled like old bones
along the threadbare hours,
slow time stretched and thrust forward
On fast spinning wheels.

Nights were black and white,
Crumpled as newsprint,
Damper than fish, more
Empty than a beer-stained glass.
While the world fled from us,
Cars and stars gone like gnats
Through reflective panes.

The port was all wetness
Tired bodies moving toward
Another plane. Aimless
Luggage stood silver-stretched

by lamplight, or on metal trollies,
Waiting to be conjured, claimed
And given purpose.

Mornings were full fat
Camembert, and rich
with languages and coffee
The clamorous coins in our pockets
Now less alien. I listened to Ockeghem
on my Walkman.

One time I found a watch,
Made for a larger wrist than mine,
on the back seat, and the driver said
Keep it – after the announcement and the
Silence in the aisles that followed it.
It may come in handy. I
Should have laughed. We English
Are good at puns.

Instead I fitted it over my cold fingers,
Tips like pebbles, and felt it warm,
A slice of someone else's time
Under my donkey jacket.
And I was glad to belong here,
Stretched beyond spume, and
Magically no longer
On the other side.

EVENSONG

LOUISE G. COLE

Head bowed, gaze hung low
she steps the long queue shuffle,
barbs of razor wire boundaries
only a scratch away, a catch caught in transit
before a snatch, a glance upwards,
some heavenly thread pulling taut to loosen
all thoughts of tomorrow, of sorrow,
an opencast mine of majesty
taking her breath away
as the evening presents a Turner sunset
streaking the darkening horizon
into a two dimensional paint chart
of yellow, orange and red,
Syrian Silk, Moroccan Melody,
Cinnabar Sunday, Damascene Dusk,
smudged across the pastel blue emulsion
of a smooth spring sky,
thumb print bruises of purple
cut with slashes of vermillion
backdrop to a slip-sliding streak
of sleek-shine starlings
a union of thousands in fluid acrobatic dance
throwing dark twisted shapes
like newlywed lovers embracing the first dance.
She remembers that day,

recalls the hope,
finds herself smiling.

DNA

CHRISTINE DE LUCA

in Shetlandic

Foo wan we here, tae dis place,
dis island; an wi dis tribe? Laekly

we wir hunkered doon, hoidin
fae cataclysms, faercist winds,

fae sunless days, starnless nichts;
dan huntin wir wye nort, winterin

trowe a ice age, deep i da gloor
o caves, paintin eemages o deer,

o bison lunderin ahead, trackin a
niff o green. As caald slackent

we spleet fae wir ain fock,
gud wir gaet, kerryin tinderbox,

seeds, mony a tale; brakkin oot
a tyoch laand, steyney or sabbin.

Naeboady is a island, yet still wir
solitary, ambivalent begyetters,

wint wi boondaries. Der a hint, a gey
strynd o da explorer lingerin i da DNA,

keepin wis on da mov, untrammelled;
unique, but sib tae da hale wirld,

encodit i dat wan aerly continent,
dat first ocean island, wir genesis.

DNA

CHRISTINE DE LUCA

version in English

How did we get here, to this place,
this island; and with this tribe? Most likely

we were hunkered down, hiding
from cataclysms, fiercest winds,

from sunless days, starless nights;
then hunting our way north, wintering

through an Ice Age, deep in the faint light
of caves, painting images of deer,

of bison beating the ground ahead, tracking a
faint smell of green. As cold slackened

we split from our own people
went our way, carrying tinderbox,

seeds, many a tale; breaking out
a tough land, stony or waterlogged.

Nobody is an island, yet still we are
solitary, ambivalent begetters,

used to boundaries. There is a hint,
a strong trait of the explorer lingering in the DNA,

keeping us on the move, untrammelled;
unique, but related to the whole world,

encoded in that one early continent,
that first ocean island, our genesis.

HUNKERED DOON

CHRISTINE DE LUCA

in Shetlandic

On a wintery day, fin
simmer's dimriv saved
i da laft o mindin.
Rowe hit aroond dee.

An whan dy calm sough
is snöddit or wippit up,
du'll fin a hömin,
a maave een unrefflin

tae gowld: dat glöd
laid by ithoot tinkin.
An whan on a amp
an canna tak paes, fin

whaar du stored
luckie minnie's oo,
swaars o hit mirlin
in a laar o whicht wind.

An whan doon apön it
mind on da aald fock
– croppened an spaegied –
still game fur a reel,

second nicht o a weddin;
back-steppin laek mad
red-nekkit an pearlin,
shön dirlin an kyempin.

An whan warnin comes
ta hunker richt doon,
oppen da trapdoor
tae dy lipperin store.

HUNKERED DOWN

CHRISTINE DE LUCA

version in English

On a wintry day, find
summer's sunrise saved
in the loft of memory.
Wrap it around you.

And when your calm spirit
is twisted or tangled,
you'll find a long twilight,
a mauve one unwrapping

to gold: that glow
stored up unconsciously.
An when you're anxious
and cannot be at peace, find

where you stored
softest bog cotton,
swathes of it quivering
in a light stir of white wind.

And when depressed
remember the old folk
– all rheumatics and aching muscles –
still game for a reel,

second night of a wedding;
back-stepping like mad
red-necked and sweating
shoes beating, competing.

And when warning comes
to hunker right down,
open the attic hatch
to your overflowing store.

Note: *traditional rural Shetland weddings were typically held
over three nights.*

THE TRUTH OF US

MARTIN JOHNSON

To tell the truth of us
I'd need to use my feet:
Many dactyls merrily,
A few sombre spondees;
Stanzas of happiness,
Couplets of gloom.

A moment of doom,
Then the last full stop.

THE PHOTO

AOIFE LYALL

Face down, he could have tripped
in his eagerness to reach the waves:
to feel the delicious biting
froth foam on his bare legs; to gasp
as his favourite denim shorts slowly drown
in salted spray to quench their sudden thirst.

Or maybe he simply fell asleep on the warm dry sand,
enchanted by the gentle heat and giving pressure;
wrapped in a dream as the sea curls in around him,
his favourite red t-shirt bunched with gentle turns,
raised over the jutting hip of a growth spurt,
his faced turned, coy, as though in sleep
he sees the photos saved for future birthdays.

Just out of sight, perhaps, a mother
ready to scoop him up in tender arms
as the sea soaks through the soles
of cartooned shoes and cartooned
socks, knowing she will wipe the wet sand
from his laughing crying lips, sing sweet
low notes to soften the crash of small
swells that threaten him, and wrap
him in a sun-drenched towel to draw
the sea from his soft skin.

Only, no.

His arms are by his side.

His upturned hand, too white for sleep.

The man who scoops him up, a stranger.

THE DECISION

SUZY NORMAN

I watch as the eye in a whirlwind, my senses pitchforked;
I see her eyes narrow, his mouth open, close, open-close.
The room turns to liquid.
From the corner of the room, I hear the words he doesn't
have the requisite papers.
Arrangements must be made.
This is what they say and I try to listen.

Her coffee cup rests on the edge of the table. A single bulb
hisses above their heads.
I see it all: Their rings; their watches; the expensive cut of her
suit;
a dab of toothpaste on his collar; a grey hair swimming
against the tide of her centre parting.
Waiting in the corner, I listen to their voices:
a plucked string echoing out; a hum remaining.

WILD ISOLATION

MARTIN REED

1

The starlings   they're keeping to themselves
And who would want them   Not to?
Truth to tell   they're a law unto themselves
Well known for it   Pikies and then some
Snitch anything that's going that's them
Then gang up   Gang up and get away
Piss-takers everything – takers

2

Looking down on   one clean lone rat
by a back-hedged stream   He's groom fresh   Fur glossed
Bushy-brown   like a hipster's beard   Yes, really
Running away now   All tail-sway irrelevance
Doesn't want to be seen   Too much

3

The rooks   will refer you to their boss
But who's he?   So they remain in these trees.
Revelling as always   in their own noise
While a grey-beard   old-guard watches
for sights and sounds   to suck-still-black in
But there's something missing?   Something?

4

That background   from the road
Swish   death-swagger, judder
Morning-monster   waking at 5am
too macho by half   Heaving
Then going like   not quite loco.
– *Notice*   not nearly so much now
Tin snake   dwindled to a thin stream
A dried-up seam.   Hear – just a lorry
Climbing the hill   grumbling in its gears

5

So an earth quiet   pervades in this –
Behind-the-houses   Beside-the-road
Hollowed and widened   old hedge row
Where the kids go to smoke and play
when they're not kept in – but now they're kept in
Except for walks   with their mums and dads
In the '*proper*' parks

6

Those kids' detritus   Cans
Cardboard   even a few condoms maybe
a coke bottle   label half off   Occasionally flapping for help
All left in the lurch   to besmirch green and brown –
While squirrels   maintain their slight sordidness
Without being thought – sweet.

7

Yeeaaarghh! Ya cann' keep ME down!
A drunk   shouts drunkard things
At the air   outside the hedges
Like Pan – misplaced.
Sheeple!   All a yah – fooled!!

8

This plastic bag   snagged branch
holly bush   has its own secret life
Beside the clear stream   Keeping and purifying itself
By its own action   a just audible arpeggio
Of making its own way   Gently arguing the toss
with turf, rock and rubbish

9

Muntjac – urban semi-myth – marginally
fairy built   tusked and horned
Of the too late   and the too early
But stirred out now   in the silence   of the rook's song

10

And that's it   All seems to wait
For something   to burst in
A gust of wind   unruly earth-gudgeon   Huh!
And the leaves scuff   Cloud out slowly
Scram thin – Settle – settle

11

In the aftermath   a moth
Blown   from its bark
One wing fixed out   taxi-ing in the dirt
Round and round   like a program gone wrong
- the muntjac's gone

12

A bird flies over   and the world blinks

13

End-branch fingers - waving benediction

14

So all return   come back together
Take their places   - again

CROSSING BORDERS

ADRIENNE SILCOCK

I have plundered art galleries
shovelled up banks of wild flowers
pulled skeins from loose grey skies
to knit a blanket for your shivering back

I have watched your journey,
or the likes of it, on TV
the rough roads, the squalid camps,
the drownings.

You hunker down your hope
watch clouds unravel
dream of petals that unfurl at home
how you might have painted them

the one thing you wish for is denied
borders are more than frames for pictures
you see no edges in the skies.

JE SUIS EUROPÉEN

GEORGE SZIRTES

1

I have the badge that does what badges do.
The badge declares. Behind the declaration
a vast silence. In the silence voices
that inhabit silence as they would a city complete with
landmarks, full of silent statues that speak the city into
ordered being.

What is the city? What is the silence doing?
Whose are the voices wandering among statutes?
Where do the voices lead? Whose are the petty
quarrels embodied in a street map that retraces
its own history and turns it into fiction,
and which of these fictions should we regard as true?

2

Silence is cacophony with the sound turned off.
Cacophony is Bach, Haydn and Mozart carved
into statues with open mouths, surveying
our disasters and turning it into music.
There are reasons for living here.
There is the music, there are statutes in the streets.

There are also the dead in their brief notes,
those missing from archives, stalls and shops that close
and vanish. There is the constant background musak

we all move to in the silence without trying.
There is everything we have made and have deserved.
There is the silence. The sneeze and the dry cough.

3

I am a citizen of an overdressed republic
that knows itself as more than an illusion
and will keep donning clothes and moving on.
Sometimes I think I too am overdressed.
I think I should strip naked, walk the street
with nothing on, and face the filthy weather

we emerge from. I think I is another
as we all are. I think it's getting late
and dark. It's hard to see. I smell the dust
that's everywhere and settles. I know it mine.
I am in love. I am standing at the station
waiting to board. I'm not about to panic.

THE BORDER

SUSANNAH TASSELL

The child brushed tears from his father's face,
His grubby hands moth soft.
Please don't cry father, please don't cry,
You are brave father, so brave.

I am broken son, so broken.
There is no way forward. There is no way back.
The child embraced his father's neck,
His small, tired arms, stick thick.

You kept me safe on the wild, wild sea,
You are strong father, so strong.
I am scared son, so scared.
There is no way forward. There is no way back.

The child gazed into his father's eyes;
You carried me high on the stone-strewn road,
You said we would walk to a better life.
Were you wrong father? Were you wrong?

Our dreams are dust son, All dust.
Nobody wants us.
Nobody.

There is no way forward.
There is no way back.

UNTITLED

PHILIP TERRY

after W.H. Auden

Jetlag after a long flight,

the shrill voices of tour guides,

crowds at the ticket barrier, a face

to welcome which the Pope has not contrived

mitre or stole: it stares up at the famous ceiling,

craning the neck, and takes a picture,

and at once a figure approaches saying: "Noc *amera, noc
amera*".

A slight cough at which no-one bats an eyelid.

Rain is falling. Clutching a red umbrella

to protect himself from the sudden downpour

he walks out quietly to infect a country

whose terrible future may have just arrived.

MESSAGE CLEAR

PHILIP TERRY

Stay Alert » Control the Virus » Save Lives

Stay Alone » Control the Virus » Save Liturgy

Stay Alethic » Control Chart the Virus » Save Liturgy

Stay Alexia » Control Stick the Visa » Savage Liturgy

Steal Antidote » Control Stick the Visa » Saunter Litmus

Steam Antidote » Control Stick the Visage » Saturate Litmus

Steam Antidote » Control Stick the Visor » Saturate Litany

Steam up Antidote » Controversy the Visor » Saturate Litany

Steam up Alfalfa » Controversy the Visor » Saturate Litany

Sleep Alfalfa » Controversy the Visor » Saturate Liquidity

Sleep Alfalfa » Convene the Visor » Sanction Liquidity

Sleep Algebraic » Convene the Voracious » Sanction Liquidity

Steer Algebraic » Convene the Voracious » Sacrifice Liquidity

Steer Algebraic » Convey the Voracious » Sacrifice Life

Acknowledgements

DNA by Christine De Luca is published with kind permission from *Dat Trickster Sun* (Mariscat Press 2014).

Many thanks to all the contributors.

The contributors

Anna Johnson *ajbooksandbags.com*

Attila the Stockbroker *attilathestockbroker.com*

Pen Avey *henandink.com/coop/pavey*

Rebecca Balfourth *balfourthrbpoetry.wordpress.com*

M W Bewick *mwbewick.com*

Therena Blair *tbd_poet@outlook.com*

Mark Brayley *Markbrayley.com*

Catherine Coldstream *catherinecoldstream.com*

Louise G. Cole *louisegcolewriter.com*

The contributors

Christine De Luca *christinedeluca.co.uk*

Martin Johnson *martin.johnson@virgin.net*

Aoife Lyall *@PoetLyall*

Suzy Norman *spotlight.com/1532-4532-3730*

Martin Reed *voiceit2006@yahoo.co.uk*

Adrienne Silcock *www.adriennesilcock.co.uk*

George Szirtes *georgeszirtes.blogspot.com*

Susannah Tassell *susie_freeman@hotmail.com*

Philip Terry *carcanet.co.uk*

BV - #0020 - 040920 - C0 - 216/138/4 - PB - 9781999703035